JAPAN

Susie Brooks

The LAND and the PEOPLE

First published in Great Britain in 2016 by Wayland

Copyright © Wayland, 2016

Editor: Nicola Edwards
Design: Smart Design Studio
Map artwork by Stefan Chabluk

ISBN: 978 0 7502 9816 2
10 9 8 7 6 5 4 3 2 1

Wayland, an imprint of
Hachette Children's Group
Part of Hodder and Stoughton
Carmelite House
50 Victoria Embankment
London EC4Y 0DZ

An Hachette UK Company
www.hachette.co.uk
www.hachettechildrens.co.uk

Printed in China

Picture acknowledgements: All images and graphic elements courtesy of
Shutterstock except pp 9b, 11t and b, 18t, 23t and b, 27m and b, 28b,40t, 42t and
44b Corbis; pp 20b, 21t and 22br Wikimedia Commons.

CONTENTS

JAPAN ON THE MAP

CHINA

RUSSIA

Picture a country surrounded by sea, where volcanoes erupt and the world's fastest trains whizz by. That's Japan! This fascinating place is like a world of its own, separated from the coast of mainland Asia.

Cultures collide

Japan is home to an amazing combination of Eastern and Western influences. There are Shinto shrines and skyscraper cities, chopsticks, tea ceremonies and robots. This a land where ancient traditions meet futuristic technology and the earth-shattering forces of nature.

JAPAN RANKS 62ND IN THE WORLD IN COUNTRY SIZE, BUT 10TH IN SIZE OF POPULATION!

Sea of Japan

SOUTH KOREA

Japan fact file

Population: 126,919,659 (July 2015 est.)

Area (land and sea): 377,915 sq km

Capital city: Tokyo

Highest peak: Mount Fuji (3,776m)

Main language: Japanese

Currency: Japanese Yen (JPY)

Shikoku

Kyushu

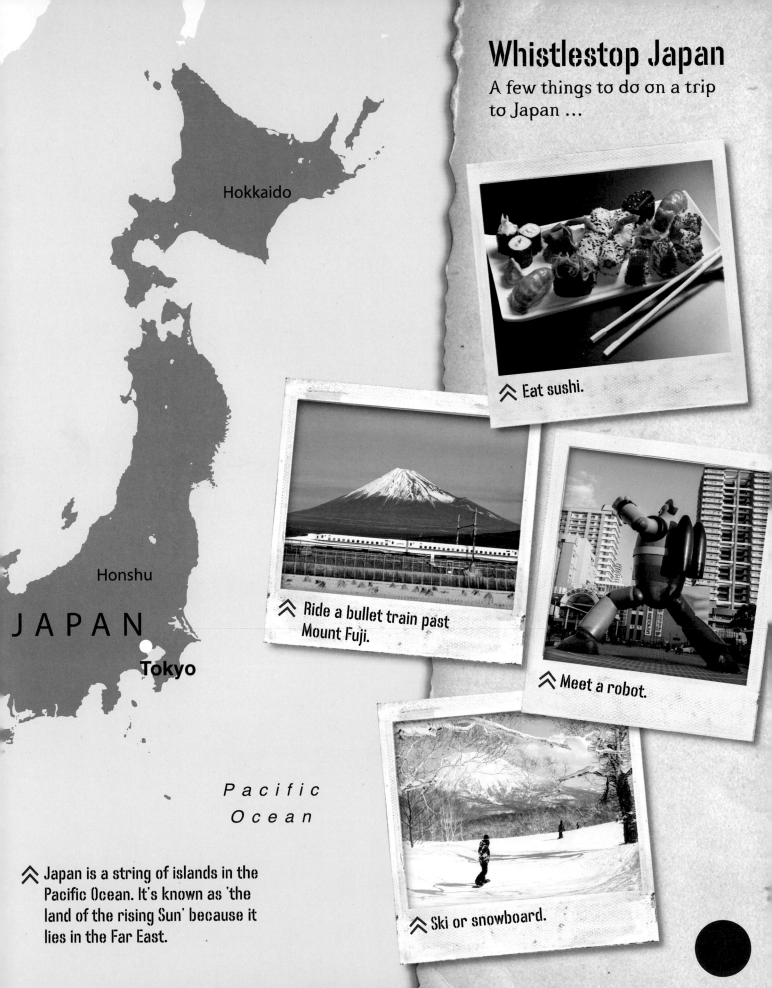

Hokkaido

Honshu

JAPAN

Tokyo

Pacific
Ocean

⌃ Japan is a string of islands in the
Pacific Ocean. It's known as 'the
land of the rising Sun' because it
lies in the Far East.

Whistlestop Japan
A few things to do on a trip
to Japan ...

⌃ Eat sushi.

⌃ Ride a bullet train past
Mount Fuji.

⌃ Meet a robot.

⌃ Ski or snowboard.

THE PEOPLE'S STORY

The Jomun culture is named after the cord markings made on its pots. ⌄

People have lived in Japan for at least 30,000 years! The first settlers arrived during the last ice age, when land bridges joined Japan to the mainland. As the ice age ended, around 12,000 BCE, the sea rose and separated Japan.

Early Japan

From about 10,000 BCE, a culture called the Jomun culture grew up. Its people made stone tools and survived by fishing, hunting and gathering. The Yayoi took over in about 300 BCE, and by the 500s CE, a powerful clan called the Yamato was in control. Japan became a unified state, led by a series of emperors.

JAPAN STILL HAS AN EMPEROR, THOUGH HE HOLDS NO POLITICAL POWER. EMPEROR AKIHITO (SON OF HIROHITO) BECAME HEAD OF STATE IN 1989.

» Many influences came from China during the Yamato period, including the religion Buddhism. This is Japan's oldest Buddhist temple, Hōryū-ji.

A statue of an ancient samurai. »

Samurai and shoguns

Alongside the emperors, Japan had a strong military and martial class called the samurai (bushi). They were experts in sword fighting and weaponless martial arts (see p28-29). Also the shoguns - military chiefs - ruled Japan for about 700 years.

Japan is the only country in the world to have suffered attacks from atomic weapons. More than 150,000 people died in the bombings. There is a memorial to the victims in Hiroshima.

(see p28-29)

FOCUS ON

☑ **MODERN ERA**

In 1868, the Emperor Meiji won back control from the shoguns and began to modernise Japan. It soon became the most powerful nation in Asia, fighting wars and claiming territory in China and Russia. The USA tried to intervene in Japanese invasions, and Japan responded with an attack on Pearl Harbour, Hawaii in 1941. In 1945, the USA dropped devastating atomic bombs on the Japanese cities of Hiroshima and Nagasaki. The USA occupied Japan until 1952, after which Japan developed as the peaceful democracy it is today.

Famous Japanese

Hirohito – Japan's longest-reigning emperor (1926-89), whose rule spanned World War II

Yoko Ono – artist, musician and peace activist who was married to the Beatle John Lennon

Issey Miyake – modern fashion designer, known for his innovative ways of producing clothes

Ichiro Suzuki – professional baseball player and national hero in Japan

ISLAND NATION

⋙ Mount Fuji is a popular volcano to climb. There's even a post office at the top so you can send a postcard!

Υou could spend a long time hopping about Japan's islands – there are literally thousands of them, though the majority are tiny and uninhabited. Most people live on the four biggest islands: Honshu, Hokkaido, Kyushu and Shikoku.

Mountainous land

Japan was formed over millions of years by two plates of Earth's crust pushing together under the sea. This forced up a chain of mountains, which make up most of Japan's landscape. The highest of all is the majestic Mount Fuji, a cone-shaped volcano that last erupted in 1707.

Water everywhere

Surrounded by sea on all sides, Japan has a massive 29,751km coastline. Its rivers are short but steep, flowing fast down mountain slopes. There are plunging gorges with dramatic waterfalls tumbling over them. Many lakes have formed up high in the craters of extinct volcanoes.

The Tenryu River flows through a national park.
»

A waterfall tumbles over Takachiho Gorge. »

FOCUS ON

☑ **VARIED CLIMATE**

The islands of Japan trail for over 3,000km, and the climate varies from place to place. In the north the summers are short and winters long and snowy, while in the south it's warmer year-round. Japan is affected by the monsoon, a seasonal wind that brings heavy rains from June to October. The country experiences lots of typhoons (tropical storms) at this time of year, often causing dangerous floods and landslides. In 2015, more than 100,000 people were forced to flee their homes as Typhoon Etau (right) brought torrential downpours and rivers burst their banks.

THE COLDEST TEMPERATURE RECORDED IN NORTHERN JAPAN WAS -41°C IN 1902!

RING OF FIRE

Japan sits on one of the least stable parts of Earth's crust - a region around the Pacific Ocean, known as the Ring of Fire. This is a place where earthquakes and volcanoes regularly rattle the landscape.

The volcano Sakurajima erupts March 30, 2010 in Kagoshima City, Japan. ⌄

Violent volcanoes

Japan has about 110 active volcanoes - in other words, ones that have erupted in the last 10,000 years. Many are very close to populated areas, so scientists monitor them all the time and evacuate people if they predict an eruption.

Shaking quakes

Up to 1,500 earthquakes rock Japan each year, though most are too small to cause damage. When large quakes strike under the sea, they can shake up giant waves called tsunamis. Japan excels in earthquake-resistant buildings, evacuation drills and tsunami defences. Even so, major disasters can happen (see below).

ABOUT A FIFTH OF THE WORLD'S EARTHQUAKES HAPPEN IN JAPAN.

FOCUS ON

☑ DISASTER 2011

In 2011, a gigantic earthquake struck under the sea near Japan. It was the strongest the country had seen, and the fifth strongest in the world, since records began. The quake threw up a tsunami that bulldozed the coastline and charged up to 10km inland. It killed nearly 16,000 people, left hundreds of thousands homeless and caused a meltdown at the Fukushima Daiichi nuclear power plant. Dangerous radiation leaked out and affected a vast area. The disaster cost Japan's economy over US$300 billion, and recovery is still underway.

⌃ In 1995, one of Japan's worst earthquakes devastated the city of Kobe and around.

SKYSCRAPER CITIES

Over 93 per cent of Japan's people live in towns and cities – so it's not surprising that the biggest city in the world is here. Tokyo, Japan's capital, has a population of more than 37 million!

⌃ High-rise apartments fit maximum numbers of people into minimum space on the ground.

Towering Tokyo

One way to fit in a record-busting population is to build upwards! Tokyo is crammed with sleek, shiny skyscrapers and includes the world's tallest tower – the Tokyo Skytree, at 634m. Crowds of people swarm the orderly, neon-signed streets, while hidden from view in the heart of the city is the Emperor's Imperial Palace.

Traffic stops and people go at Tokyo's famous Shibuya Crossing.

TOKYO WAS ORIGINALLY CALLED EDO, MEANING 'ESTUARY', BECAUSE IT'S BUILT WHERE TWO RIVERS MEET THE SEA.

Osaka sprawl

Japan's second-largest city, Osaka, has merged with neighbouring Kobe and Kyoto to form one sprawling metropolitan area. More than 20 million people live here. It's a lively financial and business centre, where big names such as Sanyo and Panasonic have their headquarters.

Osaka is criss-crossed by canals and bridges. A water bus is one way to get around!

Imagine sleeping in an air-conditioned cupboard – a capsule hotel is similar!

FOCUS ON

☑ **CITY LIVING**

Flat land in Japan is hard to find, and cities fight for space on coastal plains around the mountains. Many built-up areas are growing and merging together, forming a belt along the southeast of Honshu that runs from Tokyo to Kobe. Vast numbers of people live in commuter towns or city suburbs, travelling to the city centre to work each day. Their homes are usually small, one-family or one-person apartments, and most people rent from a landlord or the company they work for. Anyone who misses the last train home can grab a few hours of sleep in a cheap, tiny-roomed 'capsule hotel'.

HIGH-TECH TRAVEL

Japan's transport system is about as modern as you can get. Roads are good, trains are super-fast and flights between cities are efficient. The main problems come when everyone wants to travel at once!

Bridges and tunnels

To get between Japan's main islands you don't have to go by boat. Several impressive bridges and tunnels cross the sea, including the world's longest suspension bridge and deepest railway tunnel. The Seikan tunnel connects Honshu with Hokkaido and lies 140m below the seabed!

TOKYO'S METRO SYSTEM GETS SO CROWDED THAT OSHIYA, OR 'PEOPLE PUSHERS', WORK TO SQUEEZE PEOPLE ONTO THE TRAINS!

FOCUS ON

☑ BULLET TRAINS

Blink and you might miss a Japanese bullet train, or Shinkansen — they reach speeds of up to 320km/hr! These futuristic trains run between major cities and are known for their punctuality and comfort. More than 300 trains travel a day, mostly on separate lines from ordinary commuter trains. All the seats face forwards and there are two classes of carriage. The train has a streamlined nose to help it move with minimal air resistance. Obviously it works — the average delay for a Shinkansen is less than a minute!

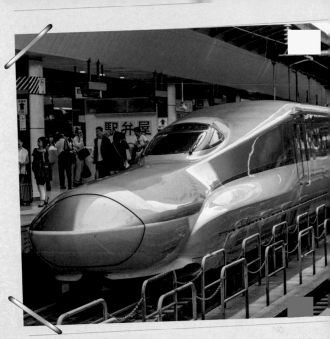

⌃ There are three types of Shinkansen. The fastest can zip from Tokyo to Osaka in 2 hours 22 minutes - a trip that used to take 7 hours!

Island airports

Where can you fit a set of airport runways in Japan? When it came to building Kansai International Airport, engineers made a whole new artificial island! It lies in Osaka Bay and is linked to the mainland by a bridge. Japan has several other manmade island airports.

LIFE ON THE LAND

While Japanese cities buzz with crowds, in the countryside it's a different story. Job opportunities have driven people away from rural areas, and now less than 3 per cent of the workforce is employed in agriculture.

Chockablock crops

Barely 15 per cent of Japan's land is good for farming, but where it is, the crops are crammed in. Japan is almost self-sufficient in rice, which is grown in paddy fields on low plains or terraced slopes. Other popular crops in Japan include soybeans, wheat, barley, tea and a variety of fruits and vegetables.

Food for the world

Japan sells many of its farm produce abroad, especially to Hong Kong, the USA and Taiwan. Among the most popular exports are seasonings such as shoyu (soy sauce) and miso (fermented soy paste), fruits including mandarins and apples, and expensive wagyu beef.

> WAGYU CATTLE ARE FAMED FOR BEING FED WITH BEER AND MASSAGED WITH RICE WINE CALLED SAKE!

Traditional Gassho-style 合掌 farmhouses like those have become a popular tourist attraction in Japan.

FOCUS ON

☑ **TIMES OF CHANGE**

There are still farmers in Japan who grow their own food or sell it at local markets, but for most it's hard to make a living in this way. The majority of farmers do other jobs too, to help support their families. There's an ageing rural workforce as younger generations are reluctant to go into farming — but some young people are taking on the challenge and thinking of new ways to make farming pay. Setting up farmers' markets, producing ready-meals and inviting tourists on farm-stays are a few new enterprises. There are also a growing number of urban farms, for example growing vegetables on train station roofs!

NATURE'S RESOURCES

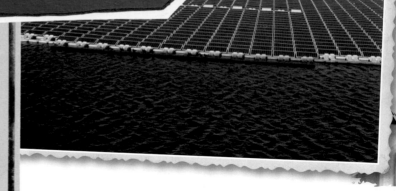

For a wealthy country with high standards of living, Japan has relatively few natural resources. It makes the best of what it's got, but is one of the world's biggest importers of food and energy.

⌃ Japan is innovative in its use of space. This solar farm floats on a reservoir, producing renewable energy without using up precious land.

Water rushes through a hydropower dam. »

Generating power

With virtually no fossil fuel reserves, Japan imports a lot of coal, oil and gas. Before the Fukushima meltdown (see p11), about a third of the country's energy came from nuclear power, but reactors were closed after the disaster. Most of Japan's renewable energy comes from hydropower dams on its fast-flowing rivers.

KIRIN

» Tokyo is home to the biggest fish market on Earth, selling about 450 varieties!

Forests and timber

Although forests cover about two-thirds of Japan, its forestry industry is small. Cheap prices abroad make imports a better option, and Japan buys in more wood, pulp and paper products than most other countries. A lot of these come from East Asia, where illegal logging and deforestation are a problem.

This bamboo forest in Kyoto is a popular tourist attraction. Bamboo is a symbol of strength in Japan, and Buddhist temples and Shinto shrines are often built near bamboo groves.

> **THE JAPANESE EAT ABOUT 30KG OF FISH PER PERSON PER YEAR.**

FOCUS ON

✓ **FISHING**

Japan has so much sea on its doorstep that fishing has long been big business here. Fish is a major feature on Japanese menus, and the country is one of the world's largest consumers of fish and seafood products. Some of the most popular are bluefin tuna and eel, but their numbers are dwindling because so many have been caught. The Fukushima disaster had a big impact on the fishing industry too, as have changing diets as Japan turns more to Western food. Nevertheless, fishing is still important to coastal communities and aquaculture (rearing fish, below) is also on the rise.

WILD JAPAN

From icy mountains to tropical rainforests, Japan has a wide range of habitats. Many creatures that live here are endemic, meaning they're found nowhere else on Earth.

Snow monkeys

Japanese macaques can live further north than any other monkeys in the world. When temperatures sink below zero, they like to roll snowballs and warm up in hot springs!

Big bears

Japan's largest mammal is the Ussuri brown bear – also known as the black grizzly. It's not to be confused with the Asiatic black bear, which has a white v-shaped marking on its chest.

Dancing cranes

Sometimes described as 'snow ballerinas', Japanese red-crowned cranes are tall and graceful birds. You might see them walking and pecking in marshes or paddy fields, or performing an elegant dance to impress a mate.

Goat-antelope

Imagine a goat mixed with an antelope, and you'll get something like the Japanese serow! This hairy forest-dweller is a national emblem of Japan and is found on three of the four main islands.

Deadly snake

Japan has many types of snake, but only three are venomous. The deadliest is the mamushi pit viper – a camouflaged creature that lurks among leaves, then darts out to ambush its prey.

☑ **THE ENVIRONMENT**

When Japan began to industrialise in the late 1800s, its natural environments suffered. Pollution from factories and habitat loss meant that many types of animal became endangered or died out. Since the 1970s, the country has been cleaning up its act and its cities are now some of the lowest polluters in the world. But Japan continues to build dams and sea defences and expand its urban areas, all of which threaten wildlife. Acid rain from pollution across the sea in China is also a problem.

FIREFLIES HAVE A SHORT LIFESPAN OF JUST 7-10 DAYS. THE BEST MONTHS TO SEE THEM IN JAPAN ARE JUNE AND JULY.

Flashing fliers

You know summer has arrived when Japan's hotaru, or fireflies, start to swarm! People love to go out at night and view these glowing bugs, which flash light at each other to communicate.

Royal flower

The chrysanthemum is the symbol of Japan's Emperor and his family. The throne is named after it, and a chrysanthemum crest appears on imperial flags, shrines (right) and even battleships.

AMAZING INNOVATIONS

There's every chance you own something made in Japan! This innovative country churns out cutting-edge technology round the clock, and its big-name brands are famous worldwide.

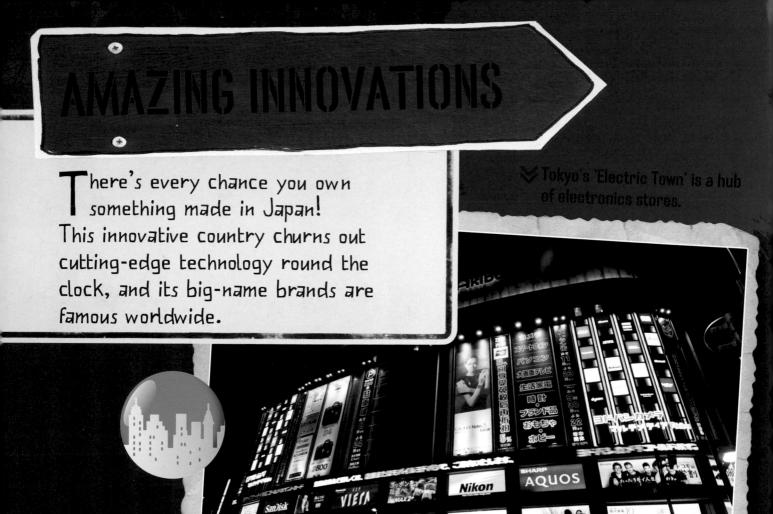

Tokyo's 'Electric Town' is a hub of electronics stores.

Big wheels

Japanese vehicles are a familiar sight on many countries' roads. Toyota is the world's largest car maker, and Nissan, Honda, Suzuki and Mazda aren't far behind. Japan is developing self-drive cars, solar cars and other eco-vehicles that could shape the future of travel.

The Nissan autonomous car will drive itself!

Powered by the sun – a Tokai solar car.

Excellent electronics

Sony, Panasonic, Toshiba, Hitachi, Canon, Nintendo – they all come from Japan! You can rely on them for brand new technology, and the latest developments on anything from cameras and smartphones to games consoles and TVs.

Inventing the unuseless

Japanese invention isn't all serious. Chindogu is the art of creating 'unuseless' solutions to everyday problems – or you could just never end up using it (it doesn't count). Examples of chindogu include sweeper shoes (with a dustpan and brush attached) and the chopstick fan (clips on to chopsticks to cool down your food).

IN JAPAN'S AUTOMOTIVE INDUSTRY, AROUND 1,600 WORKERS IN EVERY 10,000 ARE ROBOTS!

⌄ Robots get to work in a car factory.

FOCUS ON

☑ ROBOT WORLD

Most of the companies mentioned here have a hand in devising robots – humanoid, animal, industrial, you name it. Look out for robot housekeepers, shop assistants, factory workers, astronauts… even schoolteachers! In 2015, the first robot-staffed hotel opened at a Japanese theme park. Care robots include one by Panasonic that changes from a bed to a wheelchair. Robots are also being developed to perform surgery, work in disaster recovery and explore space. There are even factories in Japan where robots build other robots!

TRADITIONAL CUSTOMS

The Japanese may have a futuristic outlook, but they still cling to age-old traditions. One of these is bowing when greeting someone, which shows the importance of honour and respect.

IN THE 1920S THERE WERE 80,000 GEISHAS; NOW THERE MAY BE FEWER THAN 1,000.

Ikebana

Flower arranging, or ikebana, has been an art form in Japan for centuries. It's all about feeling close to nature and working in silence to appreciate it. People choose their flowers, stems and leaves very carefully, arranging them in a way that creates harmony with their surroundings.

⌃ Ikebana emphasises the graceful lines and shapes of stems, leaves and blooms.

Chanoyu – the tea ceremony

Preparing and serving green tea for guests is an old tradition. The idea is to welcome your visitors and treasure every moment of time spent. The host performs a ritual movement, placing everything in a certain way. Before drinking the tea, guests are given sweets to counter the bitter taste.

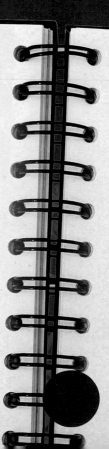

FOCUS ON

☑ GEISHAS

Geishas are a type of female artist-entertainer, once hugely popular in Japan. Now there are far fewer of them, and they perform mainly for tourists and businessmen. Geishas train intensively from a young age, mastering skills in music, dance, art, poetry, the tea ceremony, flower arranging and conversation. They learn how to select and wear precious kimonos, create elaborate hairstyles and paint their faces white. One important aspect of being a geisha is mystery and intrigue, and the girls were traditionally highly paid as companions to wealthy men.

ALL SORTS OF SPORTS

Japan is well known for its sumo and judo (see pp28-29), but the favourite sport here is baseball! The Japanese enjoy loads of other sports too, from football and golf to skiing and surfing.

Japan's hundreds of ski resorts receive an average of 10 to 18m of snow each season. ⌄

Baseball bonanza

Japan is yakyu (baseball) crazy! Children play it from an early age, and the best go on to compete on national TV in the All-Japan High School Baseball Championship. Japan's professional baseball leagues are incredibly popular, with big companies sponsoring the teams. The end-of-season play-offs are some of the most exciting events of the year.

⌄ A baseball match takes place at Hiroshima's Mazda Zoom-Zoom Stadium.

Japanese football

Football comes hot on the heels of baseball in Japan. Teams compete in the popular J-league, and many players have moved to European leagues too. The national team, the 'Samurai Blue', has qualified for the last five FIFA World Cups. There's also a strong women's side, who won the Women's World Cup in 2011 and silver at the 2012 Olympics.

Shinji Kagawa is one of Japan's top football players.

⌄ The Japanese women's football team celebrate their semi-final win at the 2012 Olympics.

JAPAN WILL BE THE FIRST ASIAN COUNTRY TO HOST THE OLYMPICS TWICE.

FOCUS ON

☑ TOKYO 2020

Japan has competed in almost every Olympic Games since it first took part in 1912! The Games have been held here three times — in Summer 1964, Winter 1972 and Winter 1998 — and in 2020, the Summer Olympics will return to Tokyo. The Japanese government has set aside 400 billion yen (over US$3 billion) to cover the cost of building and upgrading stadiums, transport links and other facilities. The Japanese are regular Olympic medal winners in their home-grown sport of judo, and also in gymnastics, wrestling and swimming.

Fans show their delight as they hear the announcement that Tokyo has been chosen to host the 2020 Olympic Games.

MARTIAL ARTS

Next time you watch someone doing judo, think of them as a samurai warrior! Japanese martial arts began many centuries ago, when soldiers learned to fight with swords or no weapons at all.

⌄ A black belt indicates the highest level of skill in martial arts.

Gentle Jujutsu

The key to jujutsu is using your opponent's weight against them, to throw them over or unbalance them. This ancient idea has developed into a range of popular martial arts, including judo and aikido. Players are unarmed and wear loose-fitting 'pyjamas', tied at the waist with a belt.

⌃ Judo is an Olympic sport.

'The way of the sword'

When samurais practised swordsmanship, or kenjutsu, they used a deadly katana knife. Today's version, kendo, involves a sword made of bamboo or wood. Players wear masks and armour to protect themselves as they fight. To win, you have to strike the other player on the head or chest.

⌃ Sumo salt-tossing has its roots in the Shinto religion.

⌃ Sumo is extremely popular, and top rikishi are major celebrities in Japan.

SUMO WRESTLERS EAT ONLY TWO MEALS A DAY — BUT THEY'RE BIG ONES!

FOCUS ON

☑ SUMO

The national sport of Japan is a battle between two enormous, near-naked wrestlers! Known as sumo, it began in ancient times but flourished in the imperial courts of the 1600s. Sumo wrestlers, called rikishi, wear coloured loincloths (mawashi) and can weigh over 200kg. Before a match, they perform a series of symbolic rituals, including a ring-entering ceremony and tossing salt to purify the ground. Then each rikishi tries to barge the other out of the ring or trip him over. Matches usually last for just a few seconds, or minutes at the most!

GROWING UP IN JAPAN

Families tend to be small in Japan, with just two generations per household. Traditionally the mother looks after the children while the father works, though more women now are going out to work.

Many children join after-school clubs or teams.

School slog

The Japanese see education as the key to success, and schools are really competitive. Pupils work long days and take regular high-pressure tests. Most children continue with high school when their compulsory education is over. Some go to cram schools, called *juku*, to prepare for exams or get extra help with their studies.

Schoolchildren in Tokyo gather at the start of the spring term.

30

Ancient religions

Nearly 80 per cent of Japanese people believe in Shinto, an ancient religion that's unique to this country. They worship spirits called kami, which include things in nature such as the wind, rain, rocks and trees. Many people combine Shinto with Buddhism, Japan's next biggest faith.

≫ A Buddhist priest hands out good luck charms.

⌄ Japan has tens of thousands of Shinto shrines.

IN JAPAN PEOPLE SHOWER BEFORE THEY BATH, LEAVING THE BATHWATER CLEAN SO THAT OTHERS CAN USE IT.

FOCUS ON
☑ **JAPANESE HOMES**

If you step into a Japanese home, remember to take your shoes off! There's usually an entrance area, called the genkan, where you leave them and put on house slippers. Most homes, even those in modern apartment blocks, include a traditional washitu room too. Here the floor is covered in tatami (rice straw) mats, and a sliding paper door called a shoji divides different areas. Furniture includes a low table and cushions on the floor, and a futon might be rolled out at night for sleeping. The bathroom is seen as a separate part of the house, where you put on a different pair of slippers.

⌄ Tea is laid out in the washitsu room.

GET THE LOOK

The Japanese love everything up-to-the-minute – and this is true of their fashions too. Young people in particular are image-conscious and never far from the latest trends.

Tokyo's Harajuku district is like a giant outdoor catwalk!

Big buyers

Japan's big cities all have glitzy shopping streets, lined with international brands. Young customers with an eye for design make this one of the hottest fashion markets in the world. Fashion magazines are a popular way for teenagers to get ideas. The cosmetics industry does well here too.

FOCUS ON

✓ STREET STYLE

Japan's streets see such a fast-changing mass of fashion crazes that it can be hard to keep up. Many young people go for a quirky mismatch of different styles and looks. Kawaii is the Japanese term for all things super-cute, and it pitches up in trends like the Sweet Lolita 'doll' look — all ribbons, bows, ruffled petticoats and bloomers. Kawaii kids choose pastel or neon colours, even down to pink or green hair. The style has gone global among the under-25s — in 2014 the word kawaii was added to the Collins English dictionary.

'COSPLAY' IS THE JAPANESE TREND OF DRESSING LIKE YOUR FAVOURITE CARTOON OR GAMING CHARACTER!

⌃ The Lolita look is influenced by Alice in Wonderland and Victorian Britain!

⌃ Japanese designer Yumi Katsura joins her models on the catwalk.

Designer names

Comme des Garçons might not sound Japanese, but it is! It's one of many successful fashion labels that have spread from this country around the world. Issey Miyake is probably the most famous Japanese fashion designer, while Uniqlo is known globally for its current, affordable clothes.

⌃ You've got to be quirky to carry off cosplay!

WORK AND LEISURE

Hard work and loyalty are deeply ingrained in the Japanese culture. People dedicate themselves to their jobs almost as much as to their family, putting pressure on their leisure time.

Working Hours

Japan is well known for its long working hours. Some people even die from overwork, which the Japanese call *karoshi*. Companies expect total commitment to the job, and workers often put in long hours out of a sense of loyalty and friendship to their colleagues or because of peer pressure.

⌄ Office lights glow by night as people work late in this business district.

Company ties

In the past, Japanese firms offered lifetime job security in return for loyalty from their employees. This has changed a fair bit in the last decade, as economic problems forced businesses to lay off staff. People now change jobs more often and many work part-time or on short-term contracts.

FOCUS ON

☑ **TIME OUT**

While most people look forward to taking time off, in Japan it's rare for workers to use their full holiday allowance. Politicians are now looking to make five days off per year compulsory, to try to lessen the problems that people suffer through stress at work. In their leisure time, the Japanese enjoy things like dining out, playing pachinko (pinball) or relaxing in an onsen (hot spring). Those who have time — especially the retired generation — travel within Japan or abroad. More than 17 million Japanese tourists went overseas in 2013.

DATES TO CELEBRATE

Festivals, or matsuri, happen year-round in Japan – there are hundreds of thousands of them! Many are local events, based on a particular shrine or temple.

⌃ The traditional Shogatsu dish is osechi-ryori, served in a lacquered box.

Shogatsu (New Year)

At midnight on New Year's Eve, Buddhist temples in Japan ring their bells 108 times. People celebrate for the next three days, eating special foods, visiting shrines and temples, and giving children gifts of money.

Coming of Age Day

The second Monday of January celebrates everyone who has turned 20 over the past year. Girls dress in beautiful kimonos and slippers, and boys in smart suits. They visit shrines and party with their friends and families.

Hanami

From March to early May, Japan's famous cherry blossoms (sakura) burst into bloom. News reports tell people the best places to see them, and families hold parties among the trees.

Gion Matsuri

In Kyoto, the month of July is dedicated to Gion Matsuri. The highlight of this historic festival is a grand parade of floats known as 'Yamaboko Junko'.

Tanabata

When 7 July arrives, people all around Japan write wishes on narrow strips of coloured paper and hang them on trees and in the streets. This tradition is based on a legend about two stars that meet just once a year.

Shichi-go-san

On 15 November, it's the turn of 3- and 7-year-old girls and 3- and 5-year-old boys to be honoured! People pray for their health at Shinto shrines, and parents buy chitose-ame, or 'thousand-year candy', to give to their children as a symbol of long life.

TASTES OF JAPAN

Japanese food tends to look good, taste good and be good for you! People often eat at low tables, sitting on cushions on the floor, and it's good manners to finish every last grain of rice.

On the table

At a typical Japanese meal, all the food is put out at once. Each person has a bowl of rice, chopsticks and often some miso soup, drunk straight from the bowl. There's a main dish — like fish — plus cooked or pickled vegetables and soy sauce. Other popular foods include noodles, yakitori (grilled chicken skewers) and sushi (see right).

Bento boxes

Japanese lunch boxes, or bento boxes, vary from disposable plastic containers to hand-crafted lacquerware masterpieces (left). Inside are several compartments, packed with a range of dishes. Bento boxes can be home-cooked or bought ready-made. You'll find them everywhere from supermarkets to stations.

FOCUS ON

✓ SUSHI

When you think of Japanese food, you probably think of sushi! This world-famous form of cooking includes an amazing array of dishes, all based on vinegared rice. The bite-sized portions are usually served along with pickled ginger, wasabi (Japanese horseradish) and soy sauce. Sashimi, another popular dish, is raw fish without the rice.

A few types of sushi:
- nigiri — riceballs with fish, shellfish or vegetables on top
- maki — rice and other fillings rolled in dried seaweed
- inari — rice in deep-fried tofu parcels

⌄ Sashimi is often served as a starter.

Sushi is the most famous Japanese dish outside Japan, and one of the most popular within it.

BORN TO PERFORM

The performing arts of Japan are a colourful mix of old and new. Some types of music and theatre have barely changed in the last 1,000 years, while others are ultra-modern.

Karaoke culture

You don't need to be a good singer to enjoy karaoke! It was invented by a Japanese musician in 1971 and has taken the world by storm. In Japan, the singing usually happens in private 'karaoke boxes', each equipped with music, a microphone and lyrics on a screen. People of all ages love it!

⌄ Traditional Japanese drummers perform at a festival.

THE WORD KARAOKE MEANS 'EMPTY ORCHESTRA' IN A MIX OF JAPANESE AND BORROWED ENGLISH.

Pop idols

J-pop, as you might have guessed, is Japanese popular music. It has its roots in bands from the 1960s like the Beatles, as well as traditional Japanese sounds. One strand of J-pop is idol pop, where young stars (mostly girls) are recruited through talent agencies. Their cute kawaii style draws enormous crowds of fans.

>> Tanaka Reina sings for the band LoVendoЯ

FOCUS ON

☑ **JAPANESE THEATRE**

If you like way-out costumes and special effects, you'll love traditional Japanese theatre! Kabuki (left) is a type of dance-drama, acted by men wearing wigs and elaborate outfits. They perform exaggerated gestures and use tricks like trap doors and revolving stages. Another all-male, musical theatre style is Noh, where the lead actor puts on masks to represent different characters. Bunraku is a puppet theatre with music and a narrator who speaks all the parts. The people handling the puppets are in full view, but they wear black so they don't stand out.

CREATIVE CULTURE

Japan is well known for its traditional arts, from calligraphy to origami. Blend them with modern manga and anime, and you get a buzzing creative scene that's catching eyes around the world!

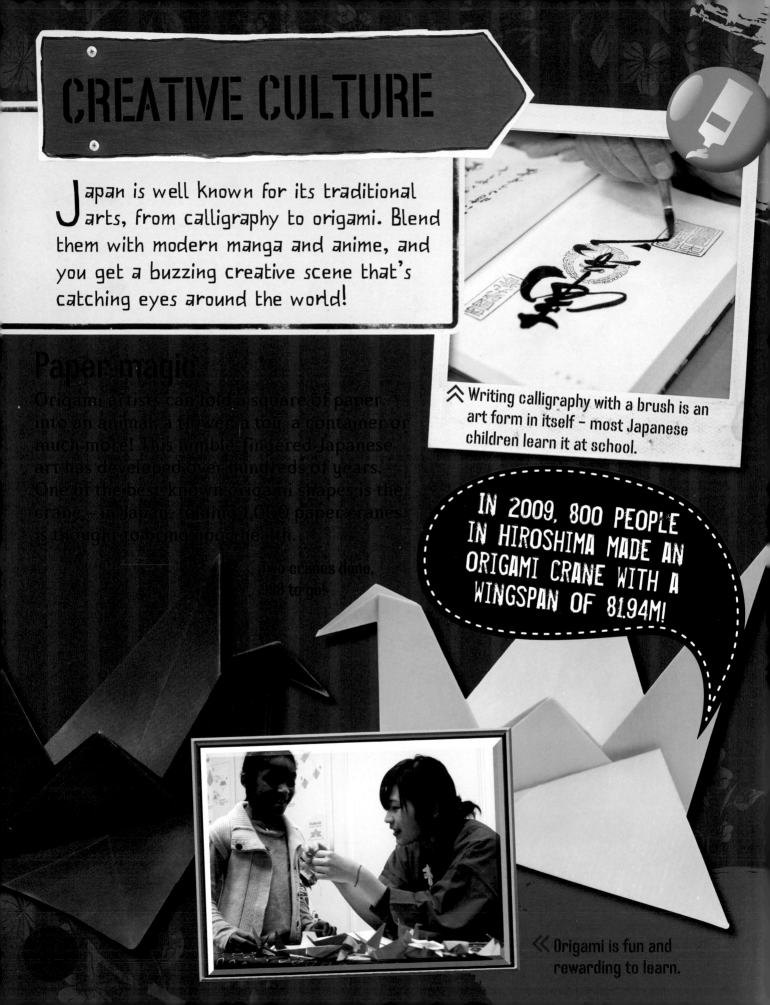

⌃ Writing calligraphy with a brush is an art form in itself – most Japanese children learn it at school.

Paper magic

Origami artists can fold a square of paper into an animal, a flower, a toy, a container or much more! This nimble-fingered Japanese art has developed over hundreds of years. One of the best-known origami shapes is the crane – in Japan, folding 1,000 paper cranes is thought to bring good health.

Two cranes done, 998 to go!

IN 2009, 800 PEOPLE IN HIROSHIMA MADE AN ORIGAMI CRANE WITH A WINGSPAN OF 81.94M!

≪ Origami is fun and rewarding to learn.

Woodcut prints

In the 1800s, the Japanese artists Hokusai and Hiroshige made famous a style called ukiyo-e. They carved decorative images into blocks of wood then printed them onto paper. The prints, often showing landscapes or scenes of life in Japan, had a big influence on modern European painting.

One of Hokusai's beautiful woodcut prints that made him famous in and beyond the world.

Manga are popular too: children, you'll come across reading the comic con characters as they...

FOCUS ON

✓ MANGA & ANIME

If you've never read a manga comic, you probably know someone who has! Modern manga began in Japan in the 1900s, and is now a global hit. There are many styles of illustration, but one of the most popular shows characters with extra-large eyes or other exaggerated features. Another thing you'll notice is that you read the stories from back to front and right to left, just like Japanese writing. Manga in animated form is known as anime, and characters from the stories have also burst into the worlds of gaming, fashion, freebie toys and other merchandising (right).

JAPAN TODAY

Japan has faced some huge challenges in recent years, with crippling natural disasters and recession. But its economy is growing, and winning the Olympic bid has helped to cheer people up.

Getting old

Japan has one of the highest life expectancies in the world, but also a very low birth rate. This means that the population is both decreasing and ageing rapidly, and there aren't enough young people to provide for the old. More than a quarter of the population is over 65, and this is set to reach a third by 2035.

ON AVERAGE, WOMEN IN JAPAN LIVE TO 87, AND MEN TO THE AGE OF 80.

« This hot spring resort is one of Japan's many tourist attractions..

FOCUS ON

☑ **LOOKING AHEAD**

Japan is a small country, but it plays a big part on our planet. Although it faces strong competition from countries like China, it is still a powerful economy — the third largest in the world. It has shown amazing resourcefulness in dealing with massive disasters, such as the 2011 earthquake and tsunami. Japan has good relations with other nations, helping it to secure vital imports of food and energy and trade its own exports around the globe. Opening up to more foreign immigrants may be one way to tackle the problem of the country's ageing workforce.

⤊ Recovering from tsunami damage like this takes many years.

QUIZ

How much do you know about Japan's land and people? Try this quick quiz and find out!

1 What is the capital of Japan?
a) Osaka
b) Tokyo
c) Kyoto

2 What is the Japanese currency?
a) Euro
b) Dinar
c) Yen

3 Which of these volcanoes is in Japan?
a) Vesuvius
b) Fuji
c) Krakatoa

4 Which Japanese theatre style involves puppets?
a) Noh
b) Kabuki
c) Bunraku

5 What is a Shinkansen?
a) A hot spring
b) A bullet train
c) A type of robot

6 What is Japan's favourite sport?
a) Karate
b) Baseball
c) Football

7 Which flower is the symbol of the Japanese Emperor?
a) Lotus
b) Lily
c) Chrysanthemum

8 What is the name of the traditional Japanese straw mat?
a) Tatami
b) Washitsu
c) Mawashi

9 What is ikebana?
a) A tea ceremony
b) A style of music
c) Flower arranging

10 What is tossed on the ground before a sumo match?
a) Sand
b) Salt
c) Rice

11 Which is Japan's biggest island?
a) Honshu
b) Hokkaido
c) Shikoku

12 What is sashimi?
a) Expensive beef
b) Raw fish
c) Soy sauce

True or false?
1) More Japanese people live in cities than the countryside.
2) Sumo wrestlers eat eight meals a day.
3) The Japanese serow is a deadly snake.

Answers:1 b, 2c, 3b, 4c, 5b, 6b, 7c, 8a, 9a, 10a, 11a, 12b; True or False? 1T, 2F,3F

GLOSSARY

atomic bomb
A highly destructive weapon that explodes using nuclear energy.

bamboo
A type of woody grass.

camouflaged
Blending in with particular surroundings.

clan
A group of interrelated families.

deforestation
Clearing an area of forest or trees.

democracy
A country that is governed by elected leaders.

estuary
The mouth of a large river where it meets the ocean tide.

evacuate
To move people from a place of danger to somewhere safe.

exports
Goods or services that are sold abroad.

extinct
volcano One that has not erupted for at least 10,000 years and is not expected to erupt again.

humanoid
Resembling a human being.

hydropower
Energy generated by water rushing through turbines.

ice age
A long period in Earth's history when ice covered much of the planet.

immigrant
A person who arrives in a place to live.

imports
Goods or services that are bought in from abroad.

innovative
Original or inventive, involving new ideas.

lacquerware
Decorative items, usually made of wood, that have been coated with lacquer, a type of varnish.

landslide
A mass of earth or rock that collapses from a mountain or cliff.

life expectancy
The average age people are expected to live to.

recession
A period when the economy suffers.

rural
Relating to the countryside as opposed to towns.

shrine
A structure that marks a holy or sacred place.

tsunami
A series of large, powerful ocean waves, usually the result of an earthquake.

urban
Relating to towns or cities.

Further information

Books

Discover Countries: Japan by Susan Crean (Wayland, 2012)

Countries in Our World: Japan by Jim Pipe (Franklin Watts, 2011)

Fearless Warriors: Samurai by Rupert Matthews (Franklin Watts, 2016)

Planet in Peril: Tsunami Surges by Cath Senker (Wayland, 2015)

The Where on Earth? Book of Volcanoes and Earthquakes by Susie Brooks (Wayland, 2015)

Catastrophe! Earthquake Disasters by John Hawkins (Franklin Watts, 2014)

Websites

www.lonelyplanet.com/japan
A detailed travel guide to Japan.

web-japan.org/kidsweb
Explore Japan and its culture.

www.timeforkids.com/destination/japan
Includes a timeline and language section.

www.infoplease.com/science/weather/japan-tsunami-2011.html
Info about the 2011 earthquake and tsunami.

www.japan-guide.com
Plan your Japan trip here!

Index